Copyright © 2011 Leading Edge

All rights reserved. No part of this book may be used or reproduced by any means, graphic, electronic, or mechanical, including photocopying, recording, taping or by any information storage retrieval system without the written permission of the publisher except in the case of brief quotations embodied in critical articles and reviews.

Balboa Press books may be ordered through booksellers or by contacting:

Balboa Press
A Division of Hay House
1663 Liberty Drive
Bloomington, IN 47403
www.balboapress.com
1-(877) 407-4847

Because of the dynamic nature of the Internet, any web addresses or links contained in this book may have changed since publication and may no longer be valid. The views expressed in this work are solely those of the author and do not necessarily reflect the views of the publisher, and the publisher hereby disclaims any responsibility for them.

Any people depicted in stock imagery provided by Thinkstock are models, and such images are being used for illustrative purposes only.
Certain stock imagery © Thinkstock.

ISBN: 978-1-4525-3901-0 (sc)

Library of Congress Control Number: 2011915687

Printed in the United States of America

Balboa Press rev. date: 9/14/2011

Best seller, best seller, The Father's Playbook

Opportune time to get a good look

A look at His style, His humor, his grace

His laughter, His presence, His beauty, His pace

In the playbook of The Dad

Said I made joy to contrast sad

Curse it not, nor disagree

Bless the All, the place to be

When you praise game, you praise Me

And when you don't, I say I see

You come and you go as you wish

What's up with Fridays and eating the fish

Playwright

You are living a story that you created.

A playwright asleep and dreaming sedated.

Dreaming of living out his own script.

A powerful pen, and the ink that he dipped.

You can play out the script to the bitter sad end,

But you've been there before again and again.

The ending's predictable, always the same.

One day you awaken, you realize "nice game".

The Holy Allow

Next topic is want, another is need.

Kinda the same, related in deed.

Can't have and want, and here is why:

Simple rules always apply.

What you put out always comes back.

When you want and you need, you're saying you lack.

Instead, think "I have" or "It's coming now".

Thankful deliverance, The Holy Allow.

Two part riddle, one part new.

What you do unto others you do unto you.

One part done, both parts true.

What you fail to do for others you fail to do for you.

Money

All of the angels come to me thanks.

Help me have money stored in the banks.

Help me have plenty, plenty to share.

To use in my life to show that I care.

Help me give freely of money and time.

Thank God He is funny and in charge of the rhyme.

The Moment

The topic, The Moment, why it was created

The subject has been pondered, mulled over, debated

The Moment a gift, a gift from who?

Bigger, Broader, Wider View

In The Moment you have a choice

Go with what you got, or hear Love's Voice

Alignment with All, The One, Holy Spirit

Calling it forth by choosing to hear it

We are writing a book that's already written

Another look of how good you are sittin'

Sittin' with The Father, sittin' real nice

Playing with The Father's loaded dice

The book that this is was written before

A collection of words from the home store

People will read, some will shout

Fulfilling in deed, the turnabout

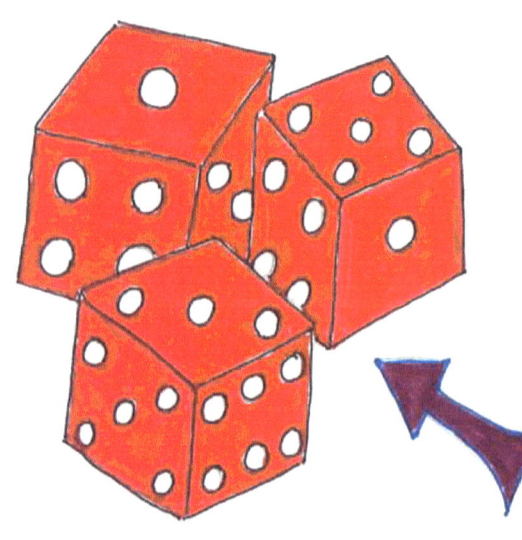

← THE FATHER'S LOADED DICE

Universal Law

Be grateful before and for the creation

Tuning in appreciation

Thankful, thankful is saying it is there

Powerful tool, thank you now share

Good idea for when you pray

And what you choose now give away

To remember the laws, share them with others

The others are sisters, mothers, and brothers

Thank you, thank you, it's on the way

Universal law I heard him say

Leading Edge

The question posed by everyone
The answers loaded in my gun
Why it takes so very long
For what I choose to come along

The reason you have not gotten
What you desire is you are not in
Vibrational harmony
With what it is for it to be

OUT ON THE LEADING EDGE

So raise your glass and down the hatch
For it to come gotta be a match
You and I the intervention
Manifest by your intention

Understand the knowing how
First you ask then you allow
In between Source says yes
Nothing more and nothing less

Something now good to know
It's all there in escrow
So bit by bit and piece by piece
Up to you to release… the thought

RELEASE RESISTANT THOUGHT

What you call resistant thought
The only reason you are not
Having now what you desire
Living a life that you aspire

OUT ON THE LEADING EDGE

Touchdown 6   Extra Point   7

Life is like a football team in heaven

I am The Coach, and you are the quaterback

I call the play, see through the lack

Lack is false, so it can't be

When you see it, remember Me

Celebration

Day by day I get to the pad

And write the words from dear ole Dad

Today's subject or dissertation

How to activate celebration

You activate with your attention

The things you think, the things you mention

So think and say and activate

The things you choose to celebrate

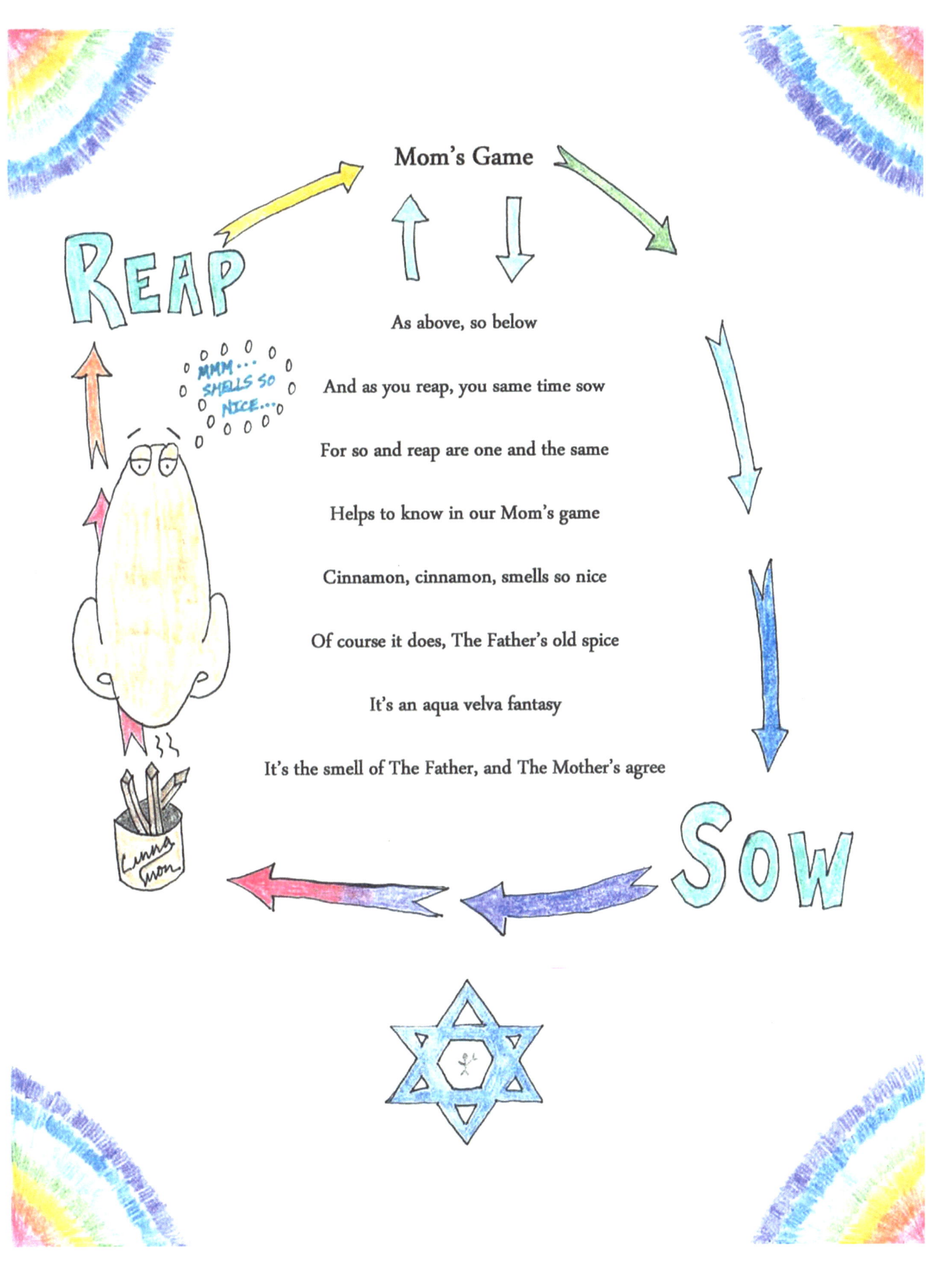

There is Much You Can Do

Behold the darkness, curse it not.

You can remember what you forgot.

Be a light on the dark, and shine before man.

Remember the Ark, and know that you can.

My sheep are lost, and now must be found.

Be ye therefore good shepherds, and turn it around.

Lead them home, lead them free.

Lead my sheep back home to me.

Mom

Our Mom made spaghetti, our Mom made us cake

The Rubbles like Betty and Barney She make

You may even say our Mom is the bomb

She is crystal, and she is the dom

Her party is rockin', Her dance floor is large

She deejays the "clockin", our Mom is in charge

My Mother is happy that I am Her son

She and my Pappy, the moon and the sun

There is Enough

About enough, clear up the confusion.

Insufficient funds, another illusion.

A digital output, it's a projection.

A sure sign of being in disconnection.

Connection is a choice, begins with decision.

Choosing your thoughts with God-like precision.

Making feeling good #1.

Relax on the way, you'll never be done.

Think and speak of things that are pleasant.

Using the moment, the gift, or the present.

Impermanence

Tattoo, tattoo, makes you think.
What makes it permanent, permanent ink.
Yet nothing's forever except for our Dad.
Our loving Father who never gets mad.
He said, 'Go, be, whatever you want'.
1st and ten, it's okay to punt.
Punt on 1st down?   What did you say?
I said it's okay to have it your way.
Your way is My way, my promise to you,
I am with you whatever you do.
Wherever you go, wherever you stand.
I am the glove and your helping hand.
So raise your hand and tell the glory.
The glory of me, a true love story.

Polarization of Creation

Control Panel picture in your mind
A magic way you will find

Turn up the levers to let it in
Return quite often, again and again

Repetition will help, help you see
Everything is a matter of degree

To what degree, it's up to you
And what color, and what hue

Make the adjustment on the inside
To let it go and enjoy the ride

Exercise, exercise, everyday

Make a connection to Me this way

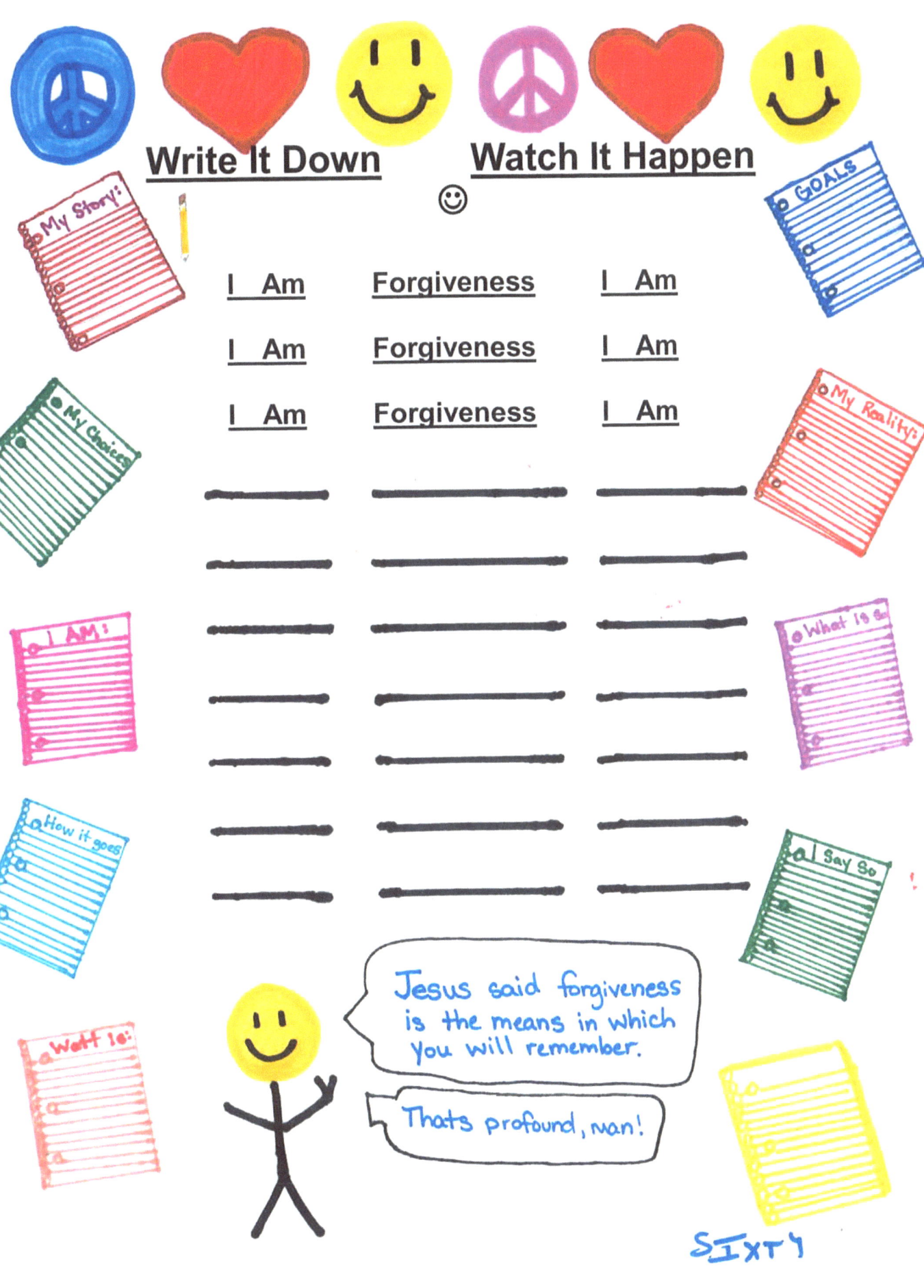

What Up?

What up, what up, The Father say
You came to earth, you came to play
You came to play a fabulous game
You came to remember, remember My name
My name is The Father, The Dad, or The Mom
It's a video game, it's a CD Rom
A game that I made, I made it for you
I made it for The Catholic, The Muslim, The Jew
I made it for all, for all to enjoy
The joy of the choosing, wow, what a toy
Choosing love, using the moment
Remembering God doesn't know what no meant
He don't know no, He do know yes
He do know more, He don't know less
But no and less must exist
For the opposite to be on the list
So all the things exist for you to choose
And by the way, you cannot lose
Everyone wins, everyone comes home
Home at last, our Dad's poem

Play From the Gap

Making the space, the space for the cause

This space is an ace, it starts with a pause

Unlock the door when you dig my rap

Sometimes it's called play from the gap

In the moment, pause the roll

Next move, now search the Soul

Ask me now to come on in

I'll be right there where I've always been

Let Us Pray

Angels, angels, Mom's operation
Only one God, only one nation
Michael, Michael, come to me now
Come to my life, please show me how
Raphael, Raphael, I say to you
Please help me now with all that I do
Gabriel, Gabriel, grateful to you
Help me keep going, help me see through

The Zohar

Zohar, Zohar, holding true

When you're ready it comes to you

Zohar, Zohar, magical book

Really glad I took a look

Of course it is, really simple

Sit right down and scan a symbol

Sit and scan, and feel the power

The Father's gift, The Mother's shower

Finding out we are meant to win

Thank you Zohar again and again

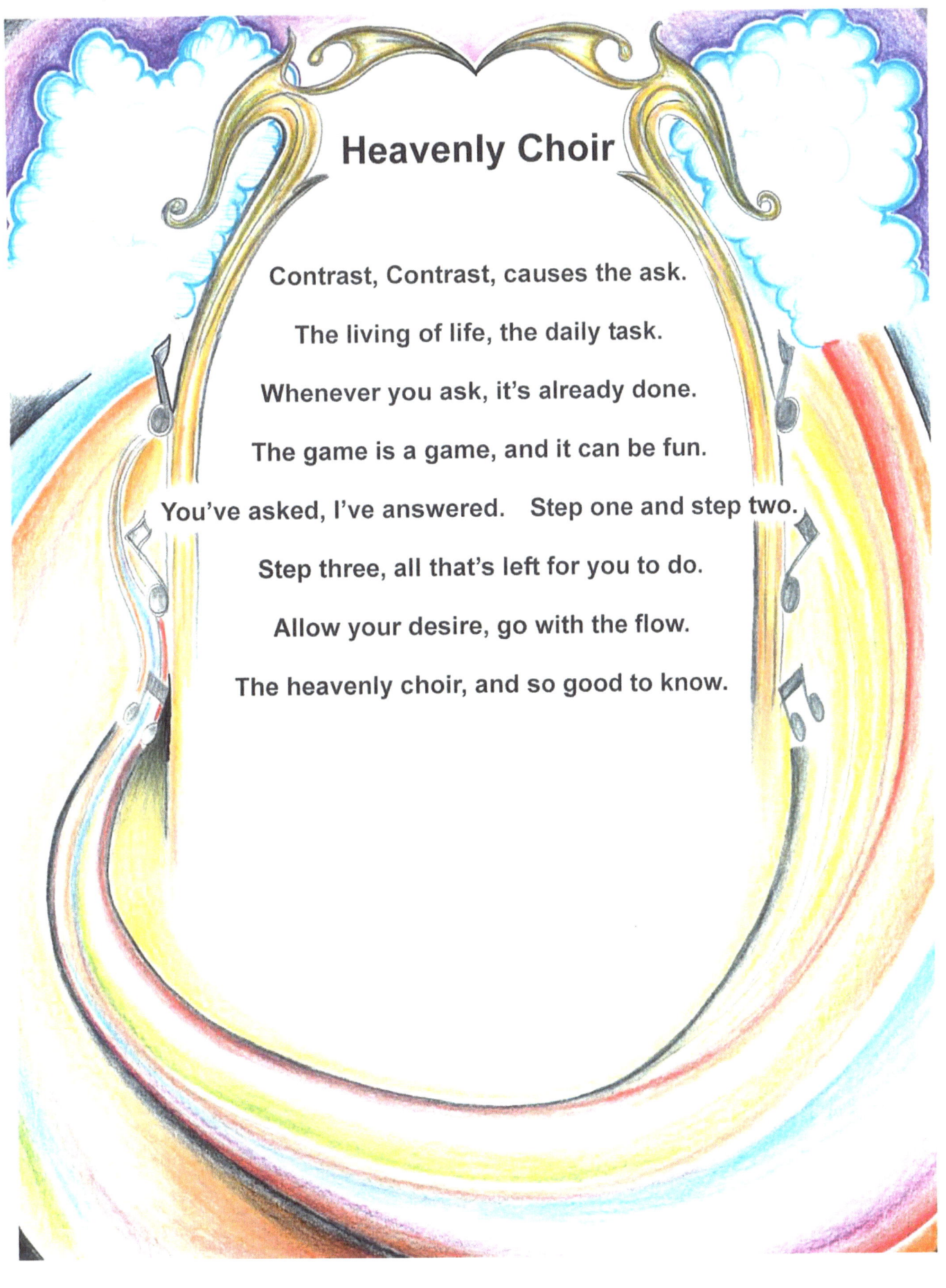

Heavenly Choir

Contrast, Contrast, causes the ask.

The living of life, the daily task.

Whenever you ask, it's already done.

The game is a game, and it can be fun.

You've asked, I've answered.   Step one and step two.

Step three, all that's left for you to do.

Allow your desire, go with the flow.

The heavenly choir, and so good to know.

A Point About the Points

In the moment you were born, two perspectives began.

Giving you vibrational feedback, Bigger Part Gameplan.

Relationship between perspectives caused the feeding back.

Perfect inner guidance system keeping you on track.

A point about the points, there is truly only two.

Who you are being in the moment, and that of Broader View.

Within is our location, we are Bigger Part.

We will help you live in joy, a perfect time to start.

Stay in contact with Us, We will more than lend a hand.

Remember when you desire, your wish is our command.

Your desires are My desires, your will is Mine.

When he knew this to be true, the water turned to wine.

In The Beginning

Here's a story about the beginning
To understand, be willing
All That Is is all there was
Tell your brothers, sisters, she'll tell your cuz

All That Is chose to know how great
Experience early, experience late
Dividing itself in one big bang
Love and fear, ring and rang
That which is this, and that which is that
That which is neither, in the middle it sat

That Which is here, that which is there
That which is neither, making it fair

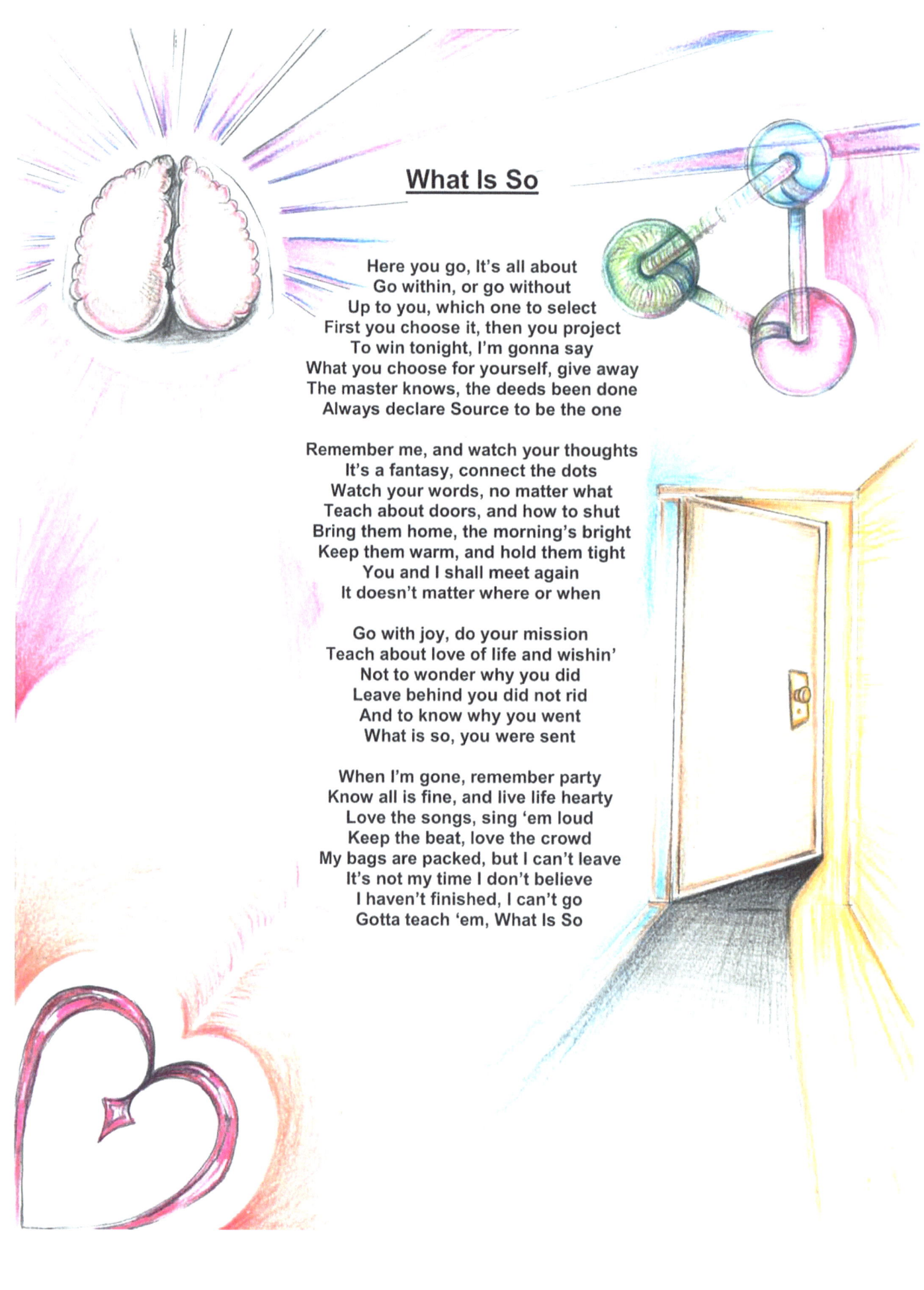

What Is So

Here you go, It's all about
Go within, or go without
Up to you, which one to select
First you choose it, then you project
To win tonight, I'm gonna say
What you choose for yourself, give away
The master knows, the deeds been done
Always declare Source to be the one

Remember me, and watch your thoughts
It's a fantasy, connect the dots
Watch your words, no matter what
Teach about doors, and how to shut
Bring them home, the morning's bright
Keep them warm, and hold them tight
You and I shall meet again
It doesn't matter where or when

Go with joy, do your mission
Teach about love of life and wishin'
Not to wonder why you did
Leave behind you did not rid
And to know why you went
What is so, you were sent

When I'm gone, remember party
Know all is fine, and live life hearty
Love the songs, sing 'em loud
Keep the beat, love the crowd
My bags are packed, but I can't leave
It's not my time I don't believe
I haven't finished, I can't go
Gotta teach 'em, What Is So

The Power of Prayer

The cars from God got their names

One was Angel, one was Flames

One was daylight, the other night

One was black, the other white

How they came?   We prayed they'd come

He had so many, He gave us some

The white one pure, and Flames is so hot

Believed we would get two, and that's what we got

FLAMES   ANGEL

FOURTEEN

Ultimate Party Bus

Here we are, another day
Doing things a different way
Deciding things ahead of time
Produced experience, cheer and chime
Just for now there is no brake
All that matters is what you make
People puffin' on a pen
Here we go once again

Hey, hey, what's the fuss
People ridin' the party bus
Shiftin' gears, illuminous
Take your turn, it's free
Ooh, ooh it's de ja vu
Feelin' like you knew that you knew
Move into the feeling, intent is key
Groovin' to the feeling of harmony

One more verse this song will go
You get back what you put out, you reap what you sow
Become single-minded, it's the cream in the puff
And you'll be reminded it's a dream all this stuff

I've been here before, gonna come back here again
I found the power hiding in the ink in my pen
Allow it to happen, it starts and ends with your thought
Teaching the teachers to remember who they are
That's what is taught

Hey, hey, what's the fuss
People riding the party bus
Shiftin' gears, illuminous
Take your turn, it's free

THIRTY TWO

Smile   Breathe and Affirm

SMILE

All my needs are met, aligned with my desire
All my needs are met, pilot light on fire

BREATHE

All my needs are met, aligned with my desire
All my needs are met, pilot light on fire

AFFIRM

All my needs are met, aligned with my desire
All my needs are met, pilot light on fire

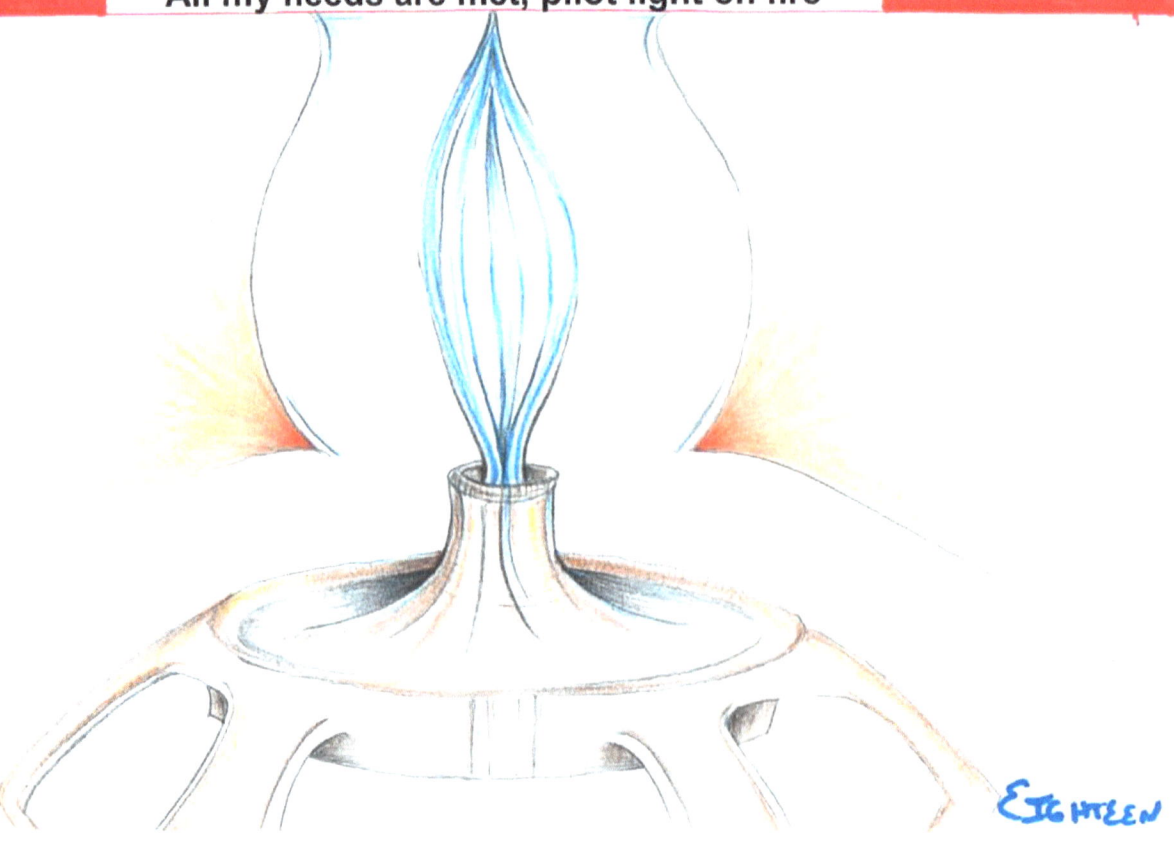

Eighteen

Top of the Hour Positive Aspects

During the day at the top of the hour

A technique for you to activate power

Think about things going good

Like Law of Attraction being understood

Easy process, give it a try

What you focus on will magnify

Five minutes per hour you celebrate

Ensures you will at a later date

Lemonade, lemonade, what a drink

Heavenly way to help you think

Clarity and feelin' great

Go ahead and set the date

The date to start, one day at a time

Then squeeze the lemons, and squeeze the limes

Concept of self is on the rise

Experience, the citrus highs

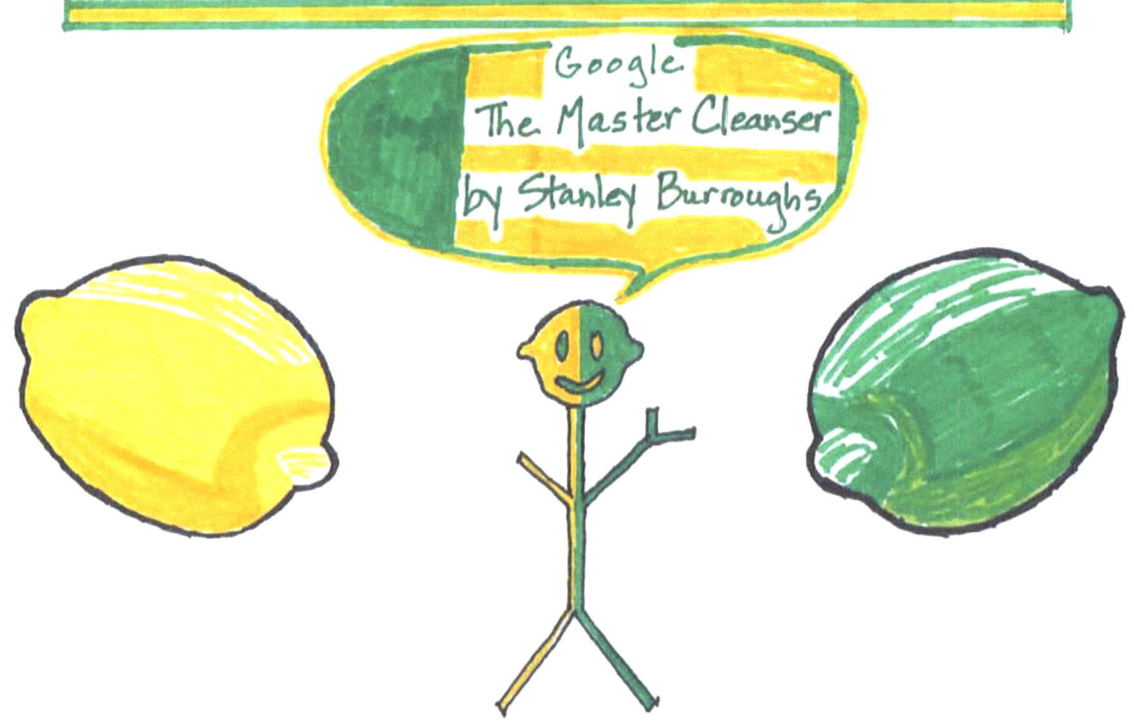

Google The Master Cleanser by Stanley Burroughs

The 42 Letter Name of God

A powerful tool, although it seems odd

Something so easy, something so simple

Relaxing and scanning an ancient symbol

Look at the page, get in the mode

Powerful symbols like a bar code

Releasing the guilt, releasing the shame

Easy to do when you use The Name

A Day in the Sun

When you are weary, fuel gauge on low
Here comes a theory, go out in the glow
To regain your power, have a day in the sun
You're just like a flower, full bloom you're the one

I will speak to you if you listen
I will come to you, so invite
I will show you what you've been missing
And color it white

We'll dance around to a sweet rock sound, dance all day in the sun
Dance around, no way we'll be bound, dance with me and the one
For heaven's sake, it's a wake and bake, rejuvenation c'mon it's free
Regenerate, recuperate, your shimmy shuffle sugar shake fantasy

What you think, you create, you become
Are you with me so far?
You express and experience some
And then you are

Dance in the hall, we'll dance in the street
Dance in the fall, dance in the heat
Dance in Detroit, dance in Bombay
In New York and Cleveland and Guantanamo Bay
Dance in Seattle, dance in L.A.
Dance in Texas and Las Vegas Hey
For heaven's sake, it's a wake and bake, rejuvenation c'mon it's free
Regenerate, recuperate, your shimmy shuffle sugar shake fantasy

Smile Deep Breathe and Affirm

I Am Appreciate.	I Am Appreciation.
I Am Appreciate.	I Am Appreciation.
I Am Appreciate.	I Am Appreciation.
I Am Appreciate.	I Am Appreciation.
I Am Appreciate.	I Am Appreciation.
I Am Appreciate.	I Am Appreciation.
I Am Appreciate.	I Am Appreciation.
I Am Appreciate.	I Am Appreciation.
I Am Appreciate.	I Am Appreciation.
I Am Appreciate.	I Am Appreciation.

Home Slice Philosophy

Forgive everyone, forgive everything.

Go past forgiveness, a circle's a ring.

A place that is clear, you may say it's very.

Forgiveness understood, not to be necessary.

Smile Deep Breathe and Affirm

Wake Up, Wake Up, Remember. Wake Up, It's All Downstream.
Wake Up, Wake Up, Remember. Wake Up, It's All Downstream.
Wake Up, Wake Up, Remember. Wake Up, It's All Downstream.
Wake Up, Wake Up, Remember. Wake Up, It's All Downstream.
Wake Up, Wake Up, Remember. Wake Up, It's All Downstream.
Wake Up, Wake Up, Remember. Wake Up, It's All Downstream.
Wake Up, Wake Up, Remember. Wake Up, It's All Downstream.
Wake Up, Wake Up, Remember. Wake Up, It's All Downstream.
Wake Up, Wake Up, Remember. Wake Up, It's All Downstream.
Wake Up, Wake Up, Remember. Wake Up, It's All Downstream.

The Gardener

Farm your own land, till your own soil.

Work your own garden, to yourself be loyal.

Think of thoughts, like planting seeds.

When they don't feel good, your garden has weeds.

Weeding your garden helps vegetation.

Letting it go with breath meditation.

Raising your levers, search database.

Remember the moment, the optimal place.

Let go of resistance, it's an attractor,

And it's the only disallowing factor.

Letting it go, you call it forgiveness.

What others do is none of your business.

People's story, opinions, and facts.

I say it again is none of your beeswax.

Your business is you, what you think, how you feel.

When speaking to Me, you don't have to kneel.

Mind On Pause

Quiet, quiet.   Put the mind on pause.

Get off of the effect, remember the cause.

The past is past, it's where you've been.

The present is now past, there is goes again.

When the ears of the student are ready to hear.

Then cometh the lips to fill them with cheer.

All is mind, Universe is mental.

When perception is kind, manifestation is gentle.

Frequency

Bigger Part, radio station

All That Is, is vibration

Frequency, vibrating sound

Another name, Well Being Abound

Broader Perspective, Wider View

Another directive point that's true

You tune to what you give attention

And something else I'd like to mention

I am responding to your invitation

Coming through by invocation

Coming soon, a Holy Meeting

I give to you the secret greeting

You say, "Hi.", and I say, "That's right."

There's no goodbye, so long, good night

Remember the song Lucky 7

They say all goodness goes to heaven

Off to hell if you're bad

Hell for making your god mad

For living in sin, for being a liar

You cannot win, you'll live in fire

I got good news, people made it all up

It was never ever true, now drink from the cup

God's attitudes, number 5

A promise to you you will not die

Joyful, loving, grateful, accepting

Count them four, and 5 is blessing

The Three Pigs

Here's the story about the three pigs
In all their glory, building their digs
One of the houses made of sticks
One house made of straw, one made of bricks

One day a stranger came to town
He said, "I'm gonna blow your house down"
He huffed and he puffed and started to blow
Two houses were down, one house to go

He went to blow the third house down, what a dick
The house it did not budge, made of brick
The moral of the story you've been shown
You can't go around blowing houses down made of stone

Nicknames

First Cause, Broader Perspective

The Unmoved Mover, The Holy Directive

G-Force, Allah, Vishnu, Source

The Father, Holy Mother, The Only of course

Mother Nature, Father Time

All That Is, Inventor of Rhyme

Alpha & Omega, The Light, The One

The All is forever, and never is done

Genderless, neither he nor she

Pure, Positive Energy

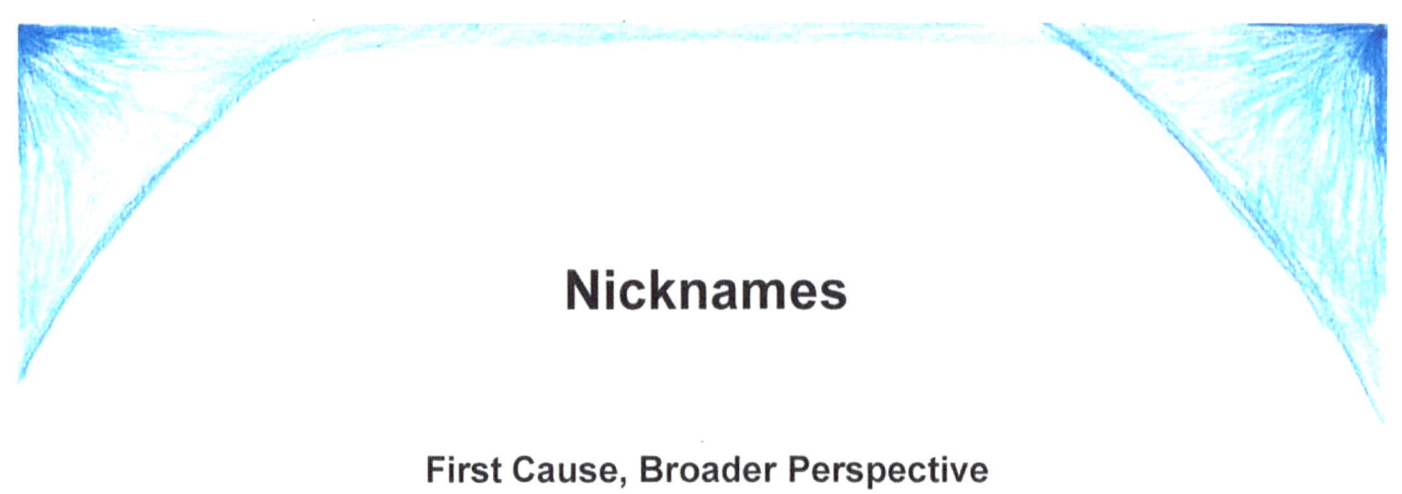

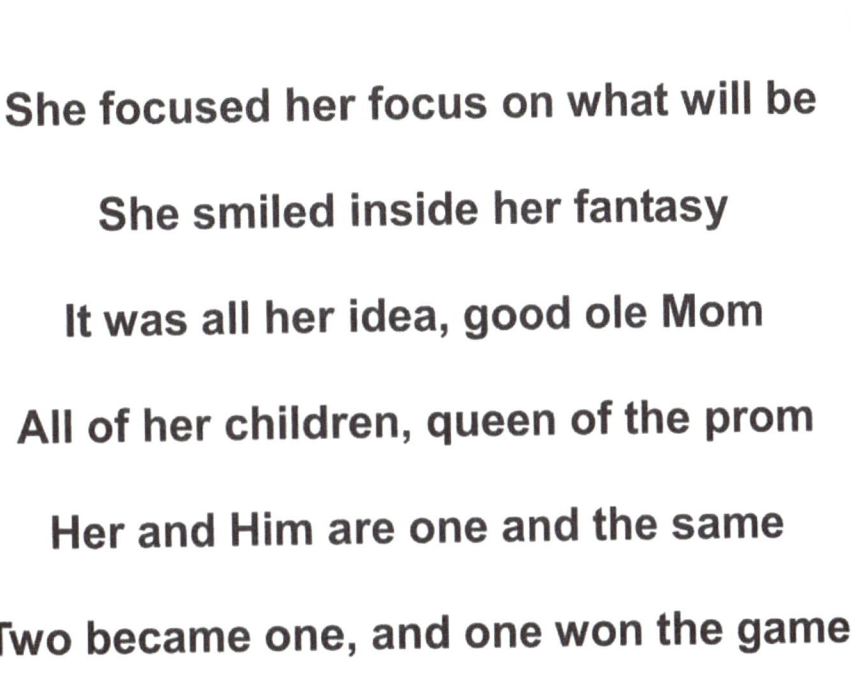

The Library

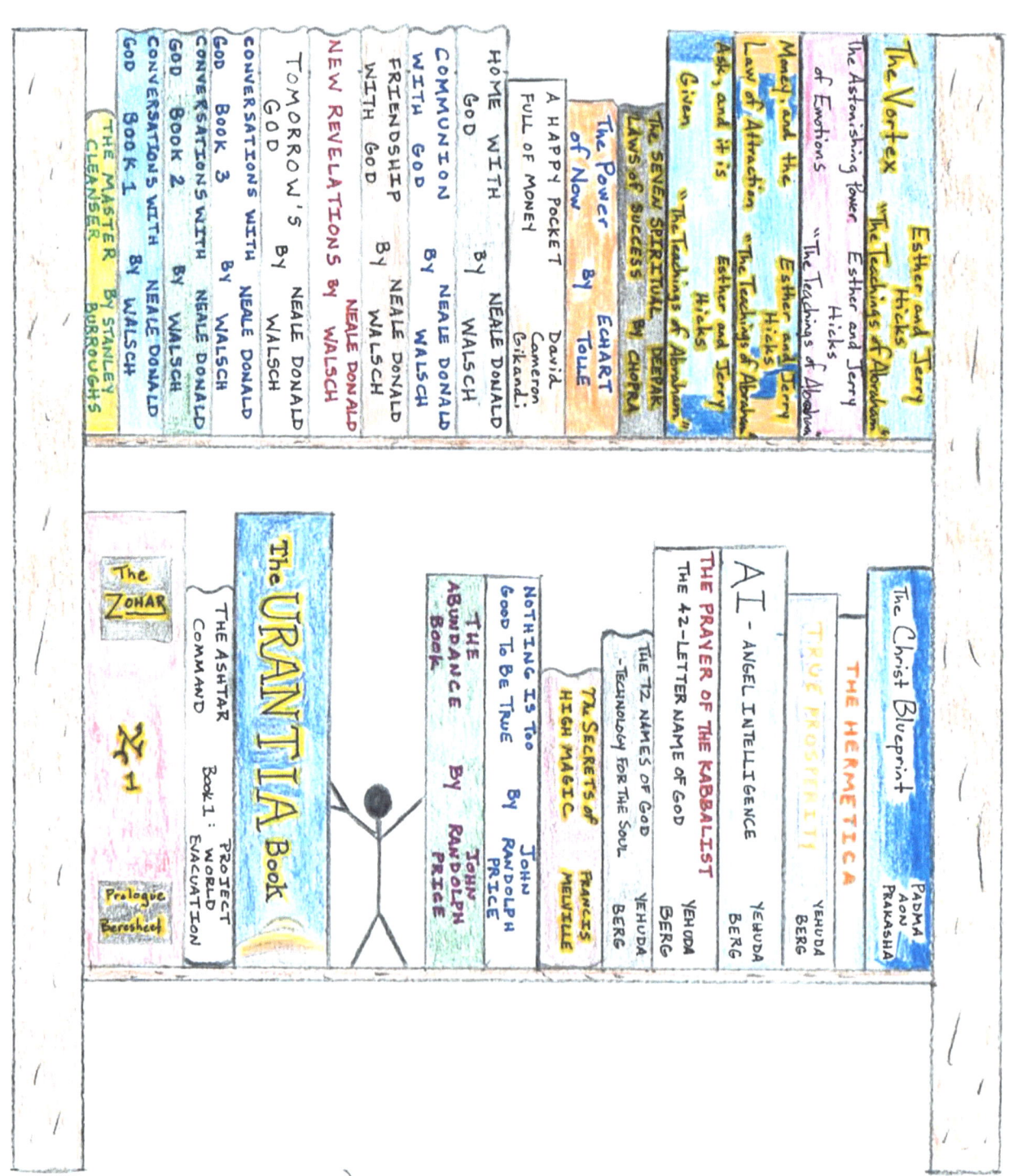

The Library

Holy Condition

Go to your favorite place everyday.

Bask in appreciation along the way.

Complement yourself, beat the drum.

Tend to your future with your green thumb.

All about your alignment, this is your work.

Not an assignment, more like a perk.

Not about what you do, only who you be.

Thinking thoughts that feel good, mental energy.

Feeling good number one, it's a decision.

Praise The Father as The Son, Holy Condition.

Joy Filled Heart

Tell the new story of your life.

Unity of man and wife.

Tell it the way you choose it to be.

Both the adorer and the adoree.

Be fun, be playful, be easy, be light.

The One, the grateful, the breezy, the bright.

Downstream, living as a fan.

Praise as often as you can.

In agreement with Bigger Part.

Enthusiastic, joy filled heart.

Grander Name

Another good one from All That Is,
it may even astound you.

The Bigger Part so loves you always,
and all of those around you.

And when you don't you cause a split,
a split of you and Me.

And when you love you'll know that's it,
you'll feel the energy.

When you think of Bigger Part,
you play a bigger game.

You go for higher stakes,
when you choose the grander name.

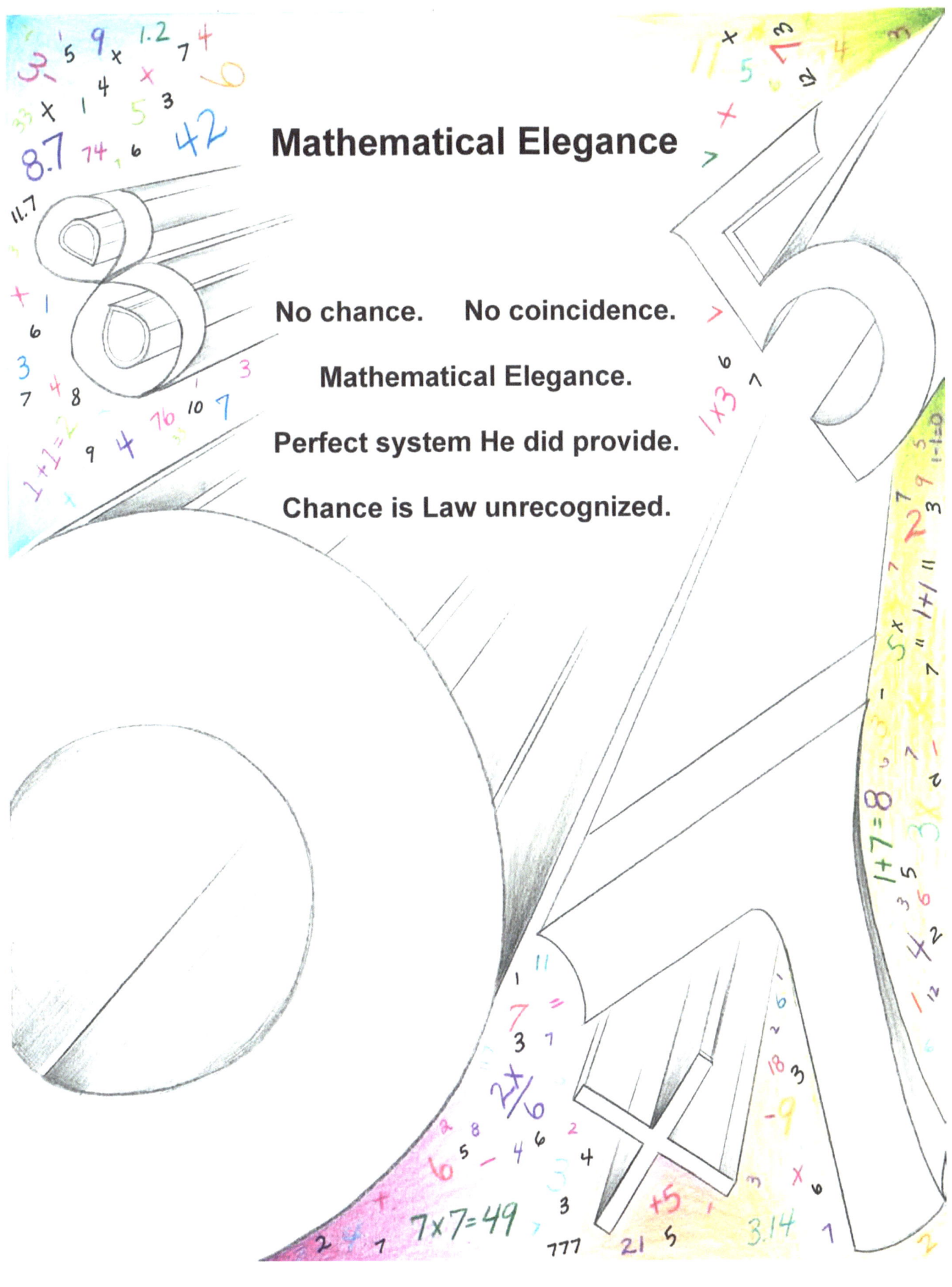

Mathematical Elegance

No chance.   No coincidence.

Mathematical Elegance.

Perfect system He did provide.

Chance is Law unrecognized.

Dad's a Gambler

I placed a bet the other day
I wonder why I went away

I thought the road and in a dome
But he said favorite, they are good at home

The line is moving, they like the fad
He's a gambler, dear old Dad

He said funny? The money? The play?
It's Monday Night Football, the play is away

Next week in college, the games of the week
The Buckeyes, The Gators,. The Tide roll win streak

Penn State, Paterno, and Texas big day
The Lions are roaring, The Long Horns smart play

The Bruins, The Beavers, and Michigan State
We easily cover all on this date

Over and over, he said is the play
The Lions have thunder, The Bears all the way

The Steelers, The Giants, The Raiders, they cover
With home field advantage, for she is my lover

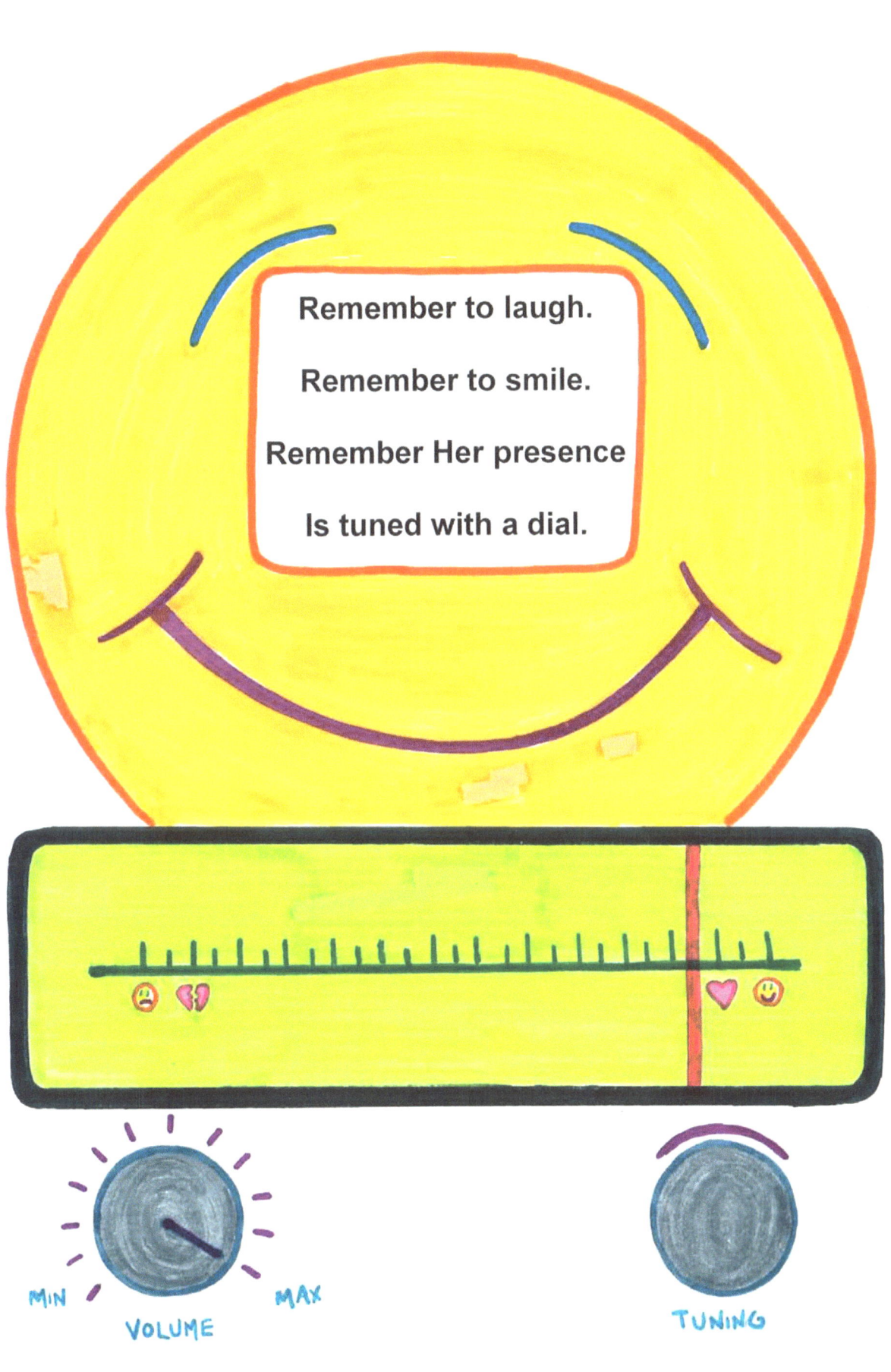

Publisher, publisher, I make a wish

He fed them the bread, He fed them the fish

Remember your promise to business for Dad

His word and His message, for you are his lad

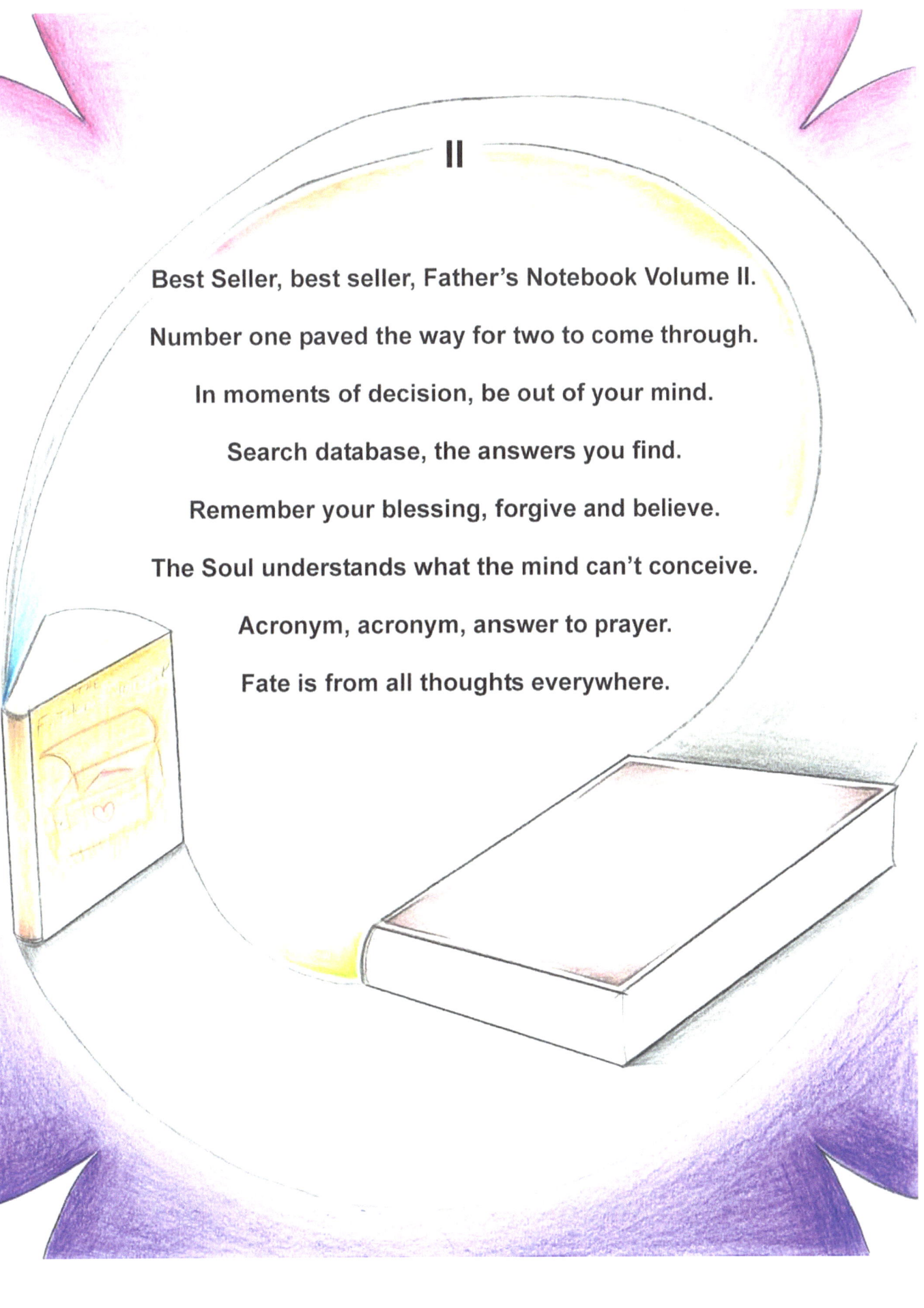

Best Seller, best seller, Father's Notebook Volume II.

Number one paved the way for two to come through.

In moments of decision, be out of your mind.

Search database, the answers you find.

Remember your blessing, forgive and believe.

The Soul understands what the mind can't conceive.

Acronym, acronym, answer to prayer.

Fate is from all thoughts everywhere.